LIVERPOOL
AND
LITERATURE

LIVERPOOL
AND
LITERATURE

By
George Chandler
M.A. Ph.D., F.L.A., F.R. Hist. S.

Rondo Publications Ltd.
Liverpool

Published 1974 by
Rondo Publications Ltd., 155/157 The Albany,
Old Hall Street, Liverpool L3 9EG

ISBN: 085619 008X

Printed in Great Britain by The Acorn Press, Liverpool

CONTENTS

1810, Liverpool Newsman, George Day
(Binns Collection, Picton Reference Library, Liverpool)

List of Illustrations

Chapter 1

Medieval and Tudor Writing from Liverpool: the Earls of
Derby and the Tower of Liverpool and Knowsley Hall;
the Molyneux of the Castle of Liverpool and Croxteth Hall;
the town clerk and the town hall.

For nearly 400 years after her creation as a free borough on the sea, Liverpool had no literary associations. During this period, its population was small and few could read or write.

Moreover, a distinctive literature could hardly evolve in Liverpool until a national language had been created.

For centuries after the Norman conquest the English had three languages – Norman French for the Norman conquerors and their descendants, Anglo-Saxon for the conquered English, and Latin as the language of civilisation.

As late as the 17th century, Liverpool's first well-known scientist – Jeremiah Horrocks – recorded his observations in Latin.

When the burgesses of Liverpool decided in 1414 – the year before Agincourt – to petition Parliament for protection against Henry V, they chose Norman French as the language, requesting "the very wise Commons of this present Parliament," to protect the "poor tenants" of Liverpool against "the officers and servants of our said lord the King," who "have come, usurped and held certain courts, by force . . . and thus the said burgesses are grevously molested, vexed and disturbed."

The earliest known Liverpool document written in English dates probably from 1411, and was also concerned with the defence of the borough's charter rights, but it is not lacking in the simplicity and directness which are some of the characteristics of good writing.

The burgesses wished to rent the right to collect the Royal dues in the borough and "poaire to tack a mon by his body." The burgesses were "halfe in mynde to take Castle Orchard," and "halfe in mynde also to gett a privy seale direct to the mayor, charging all those that holden of the King in Leverpull to appear before the Councell at London, els they will agree with the mayor."

In the earliest map recording Liverpool — that of 1331 — Liverpool is spelt Lyv'pole, and it was not until the 19th century that the spelling Liverpool became standard.

The first great writer to visit Liverpool was Geoffrey Chaucer, whose works were very important in spreading the use of English as a literary language.

Chaucer was a member of the household of Prince Lionel, Duke of Clarence, son of Edward III, who visited Liverpool in 1358, as is confirmed by the household accounts. Unfortunately, Chaucer did not record any of his impressions, and there are no references to Liverpool in his works. There is, however, a reference to a man who came from the North — "I know not where," as though this area was unimportant.

It is not until the 16th century that even a few specific details can be found of any literary associations in Liverpool. These are naturally concerned with the Stanleys of Liverpool Tower and Knowsley Hall, and the Molyneux, constables of Liverpool Castle and owners of Croxteth Hall.

The Stanleys and Molyneux maintained their own retainers in Liverpool and there was frequently friction between them, but this did not give rise to a literary "Romeo and Juliet."

A surviving ballad records the part both families played in the defeat of the Scots on Flodden Field. The ballad is written in the alliterative tradition of the conquered Anglo-Saxons rather than in the rhyming French and Italian verse forms which Chaucer popularised.

The ballad has a directness, and a predominantly Anglo-Saxon vocabulary, with a few words of Norman or Latin origin:

> But the care of the Scottes,
>   increased full score
> For their king was downe knocked,
>   and killed in their sight,
> Under the banner of a bishop,
>   that was the bold Stanley,
> Then they fetilde them to fly,
>   as fast as they might.

This ballad was no doubt one of the many ballads sung in

William, 6th Earl of Derby, described as 'busy penning comedies' and claimed by some critics as the author of the plays attributed to Shakespeare!

the halls of Liverpool for the benefit of the retainers. The Stanleys were already developing a more Latinised style. In response to a letter from Henry VIII, the third Earl wrote from Knowsley in very different language to the gentlemen of his council: "wherefore for my part I heartily desire you . . . upon the King's behalf and . . . straitly charge and commend you that ye with all haste and diligent speed do put yourself and all your company in readiness to serve his Grace."

It is not surprising that the third Earl's grandsons — Ferdinando, the fifth, and William the sixth earls, were Liverpool's first important writers. Ferdinando was praised by Spenser, wrote verses, and maintained a company of players.

William was busy "penning comedies," and is considered by several European critics to have written Shakespeare's plays.

Both can be claimed as Liverpool writers because of their military base at the Tower of Liverpool and their Hall at Knowsley.

Francis Bacon was, for a brief period, Member of Parliament for Liverpool, but there is no evidence that he ever visited Liverpool so that he can hardly be claimed as a Liverpool writer.

The fifth and sixth Earls can be claimed on the much stronger ground that they were burgesses of Liverpool, and served also as mayors. In 1574 their father came to the Tower of Liverpool, sent for the mayor, and requested him to enrol his two sons as burgesses of Liverpool. The Town Clerk of Liverpool recorded this in language more "literary" than was necessary:

"Be it remembered on the 9th day of September in the 16th year of Queen Elizabeth, the noble lord Henry Stanley, knight and earl of Derby, in his own person came to this town and borough of Liverpool . . . master mayor sitting in court in judgement between party and party. And he sent . . . to the aforesaid mayor, willing him to appear before him in the Tower of Liverpool. And master Robert Corbett, mayor aforesaid appeared before the aforesaid noble earl and . . . that the aforesaid earl requested the aforesaid master mayor to enter or cause to be entered his noble sons free burgesses of the borough . . ."

The town clerk interspersed many comments in the town books of a literary character. The early byelaws of the borough are expressed in vivid phrases. They laid down the procedure for dealing with cases of the plague in forceful but picturesque terms: "all persons that may happe to be visite with the pestilence . . . shall depart owte of their howsies and make they're cabbanes on the Heathe . . . and keape they're doores and wyndoys shutte on the streete syde as they have licence of the mayre to open thayme."

The bye-laws are equally forceful and picturesque in ordering the mayor and bailiffs to "serche the towne, as ofte as need shall require, for idel persons able to worcke and labour, or else to advoyde the towne." Here in a nutshell is the situation which has given rise to much later literature. Liverpool attracted many "foreigners" — from the neighbouring area, from Ireland, Scotland and Wales, and, later, from abroad, who were driven by worse circumstances at home to come to the port of Liverpool to earn an easier living. Having arrived in Liverpool, their sufferings created the persisting literary image of Liverpool as a city of despair.

In Tudor Liverpool there was no Nicholas Monsarrat to write a Tudor "Cruel Sea" which would symbolise in literary form the anxiety of sailors and soldiers who risked their lives at sea during the wars with Ireland. But the emotion was there and required a memorial. The Wishing Gate to the North of Liverpool, whence Liverpudlians waved farewell to their men as they sailed out of the Mersey in their tiny ships, was a symbol of an emotion which also demanded expression in literary forms. The Town Clerk was moved to intersperse in the dry proceedings of the council some comments on the dangers at sea which are amongst the earliest literary passages relating to Liverpool and the sea, if literature arises, as Wordsworth claimed, from emotion recollected in tranquility.

His account of the storm which arose in 1565 and caused much anxiety because of the ships at sea is tinged with the same emotion which gave rise to much literature in later wars: "About ten or eleven o'clock last Sunday at night suddenly sprung and rose the marvellioust and terriblest storm of wind and weather that continued above six hours or little less as well upon land as water." Liverpool's small ships were at sea on their way to Ireland "all charged with great horses, all fine apparell and other treasure!"

The schoolmaster in Tudor Liverpool was another literary figure. He encouraged his pupils to produce plays, for the records of his expenses are recorded in the Town Books. There are, however, no records of the books he used. The town had no library, but books were prized. When Sir William Norris of Speke Hall, who was for a period mayor of Liverpool, served in the Scottish campaign, he brought back with him 14 folio volumes, in which he wrote in his own hand-writing that "Edin Borow" was won in 1544 and that the books were "gotten" by him. They are now in the Athenaeum Library, Liverpool, and are evidence of the zeal for book collecting which motivated many later Liverpudlians but in a more orthodox form.

Chapter 2

Stuart Writing: the Earls of Derby; the Norrises of Speke Hall;
the Moores of Bank Hall and the Old Hall;
Jeremiah Horrocks, astronomer; Thomas Lurting, sailor.

2

Whereas in the 16th century Liverpool could claim only two writers – the fifth and sixth earls of Derby – there were in the 17th century not only the seventh and eighth Earls, who have left writings which are literature in the broadest sense of the term, but also several of the Norrises of Speke Hall and the Moores of Bank Hall. Their writings were, it is true, not meant for publication and consisted of letters and character studies, but this was true of much more famous contemporary works like Pepys's Diary or, say, Bruyère's "Caractères."

In addition to the local lords of the manor, there are surviving writings by some of the sailors of Liverpool. Collectively, these are very small in bulk, but they show an increased command of language to communicate meaning and they illuminate the workings of human personality in Liverpool with much greater insight than earlier works.

Liverpool took the Commonwealth side during the Civil War and shared the Puritan dislike of imaginative literature in general and of the drama in particular which they attacked as "lise" because they did not correspond with actuality. We have a record of Liverpool at the time of the Civil War in the diary of Adam Martindale, chaplain to Colonel John Moore of Bank Hall, Liverpool, who became Governor of Liverpool on petition of the burgesses after the town had been retaken by the Parliamentarians.

Moore was later to sign the death warrant of Charles I, and Adam Martindale was critical of his sincerity, but praised the "religious officers of the company" with whom he enjoyed "sweet communion" as they met every night at one another's quarters, by turns, to read scriptures." Their reading was disturbed by a night attack from the Royalists under Prince

Rupert, who took the town again.

The only book mentioned by title in a 17th century inventory of Bank Hall was Foxe's "Book of Martyrs," which gives some idea of the earnestness of the literary taste of Liverpool of that day. During this period the burgesses purchased two dictionaries for use in the school and ordered that they should be chained to prevent theft.

Some light on the fierceness of the religious controversy of the day is also thrown by the writings of the seventh Earl of Derby, Member of Parliament for Liverpool in 1625 and first Mayor of Liverpool under Charles I's modern charter. He personally encouraged Prince Rupert to take Liverpool and was executed by the Parliamentarians. His heroic conduct before his execution is reflected in his works.

The eighth Earl of Derby endeared himself to the burgesses of Liverpool by writing pamphlets in support of Protestantism.

Before the Civil War the Moores took part in the administration of funds for the appointment of a school master in Liverpool to teach in "any comen scole within Lyverpole." They contributed to the stipend of the Liverpool schoolmaster — Richard Mather — the famous Puritan divine, best remembered for the works published after his emigration to America. Mather was succeeded as schoolmaster by Jeremiah Horrocks, one of his pupils who also became an important author. Horrocks was born in a farmhouse near Toxteth, which had been settled with Puritans when Lord Sefton disafforested the ancient deer park of Toxteth. These farms were dubbed the Holy Land, and some of their names have survived today — Jericho, Jordan, etc.

Horrocks showed early signs of mathematical genius, going to Cambridge at the age of 14. Before his early death, at the age of 22, he became the first person to observe the transit of Venus across the moon, having calculated the time with wonderful precision by means of a simple mechanism invented by himself. Isaac Newton considered him to be among the greatest pioneers of astronomy in England. His "Opera Omnia" were published posthumously in London in 1690 — the first important scientific book by a Liverpool man. The Picton Library's copy of the first edition was destroyed by bombing, but has recently been replaced by purchase at a sale at Sotheby's. His memorial is in Westminster Abbey.

James, 7th Earl of Derby, MP for Liverpool in 1625 and a writer on contemporary religious matters.

Jeremiah Horrocks observes the transit of Venus across the sun.
(From the painting by Eyre Crowe in the Walker Art Gallery, Liverpool)

After the Restoration of Charles II the literary image of Liverpool continued to be Puritanical. It was a Quaker sailor, Thomas Lurting, who wrote the first books relating to Liverpool and the sea during this period. He describes how he was taken prisoner by the Turks in the Mediterranean and was in danger of being sold into slavery. He was, however, successful in turning the tables on his captors and, much to their surprise, landed them with peaceful embraces. This turning of the cheek was not successful in mitigating Turkish persecution of Christians and he wrote another book addressed to the Turks, urging them to exercise clemency.

Lurting was the first Liverpool writer to deal with the religious conflict arising from the increased trade which Liverpool was pioneering with various parts of the world in the 17th century — with America, the Mediterranean and Africa.

Some of the earliest surviving documents illustrating this trade are the letters of the Norrises of Speke Hall, which have been published, and of which most of the originals are in the Picton Library. Compared with the letters of shipping firms to-day they rank as literature for they included much vivid detail which would not be considered necessary now.

The following letter "to Captain of the good ship the Blessing," dated October 16, 1700, reveals the combination of piety, ruthlessness and commercial *savoir faire* with which the Norrises conducted their affairs:

We order you with the first fair wind and weather . . . to King-sail in the Kingdom of Ireland where apply yourself to Mr. Arthur Izeik, Merchants, there will ship on board you such necessary provisions and other necessaries as you shall want for your intended voyage and . . . with the first fair wind and weather make the best of your way to the Coast of Guinea . . . where dispose of what cargo is most proper and purchase what slaves you can. I hope you will slave your ship easy and what shall remain over as above slaving your ship lay out in teeth which are there reasonable — when you have disposed of your cargo and slaved your ship make the best of your way to the West Indies. If you find the markets there reasonable good sell there, if dull go downward Leeward to such Island as you shall see

'TO THE

Great TURK,

AND HIS

KING

AT

ARGIERS.

TOGETHER WITH

A Poſtſcript of *George Pattiſon's* taking the *TURKS*, and ſetting
them on their own Shoar.

LONDON,

Printed for *Ben. Clark,* in George-yard, in *Lumbard-*
ſtreet, 1680.

Title page of Thomas Lurting's book appealing to the Turks to exercise clemency in their treatment of Christians.

convenient where dispose of your negroes to our best advantage and with the produce load your ship with sugar, cottons, ginger if to be had . . . and make the best of your way home . . . but call at King-sail for orders.

Read over your invoice frequently that you may be better acquainted with your goods we have not limited you to any place, only if you can't do your business on the Gold Coast and Wida go to Angola your ship we think not proper to go into Byte. We leave the whole management of the concern to you and hope the Lord will direct you for the best. Be very cautious of speaking with any ship at sea for the seas are dangerous. Endeavour to keep all your men sober for intemperance in the hot country may destroy your men and so ruin your voyage. Let everything be managed to our best advantage, let nothing be embezzled. We commit you to the care and protection of the Almighty, who we hope will preserve you from all danger and crown all our endeavours with success.

The letters of Edward Moore of Bank Hall are also well written. His letter describing the death of his children from smallpox is a fascinating human document:

. . . but truly my grief was such, that I cannot express it and I thank God all the affliction I ever had before in this world are as nothing to it. Two days before my wife's coming to London it pleased God to visit my daughter with the small pox and when she mended my eldest son William fell sick who after five days died: a child so generously bemoaned as I think the like never was in our parts – whilst he was sick 50 or 60 people a day of my tenants coming or sending to see him. But when he was gone, and having another child lying a dying in the house I resolved to bury him very private between 12 and 1 of the clock at night.

And when night came, I resolved to carry him in my coach privately only with 40 or 50. But truly before he went out of the house there were not so little as 800 people.

And about a mile from Liverpool, on foot, the Mayor with the mace and wand, the alderman and the common council and at least 700 or 800 people met the corpse so that when we came to the church there was not so little as 1,600 people and number not seen this in man's memory as before at that church, and which was much more strange. I believe the like lamentation was not seen about us at any funeral in man's memory for there was as may be judged not so little as 600 people at any one time in the church who wept bitterly.

Truly I bore the affliction pretty well till I saw and heard such a great and general lamentation amongst my neighbours. And such a sad and mournful tone through the whole church I thought then that my heart would have broke thinking whereby I might easily perceive my loss was far greater than I could imagine. To lose him though but 14 years old had found so true and general a resentment at his grave by all his neighbours.

O dear Cousin by how much I saw he had gained in the affection of the people by so much it renewed my griefs and made them seem even unsupportable that when I came home I fell sick and kept my bed near three weeks, not of grief, but it brought upon me my old pain insomuch that all people thought I should have died.

Then in 4 days my youngest son Thomas died, who was buried at one of the clock, as the former, with many hundreds that met him. Then my wife sent her two sons that yet were to the parsonage house an mile and a half from us where it pleased God after some 5 or 6 days to visit my son Fenwick with the small pox and after 4 days he died and I buried him at another church in a buriel place belonging to Bank Hall.

Edward Moore has also left behind vivid and malevolent character studies of his tenants, in Liverpool, whom he called a nest of rogues, in his "Rental" now in the Picton Library.

Chapter 3

The Early Hanoverian period: Daniel Defoe; William Hutchinson, privateer; the pottery poets; the first newspapers, publishers, libraries and theatres.

3

During the 18th century Liverpool developed her trade links so rapidly that she ousted Bristol as England's second port, and a number of important writers began to describe her in their warnings.

Daniel Defoe was the first great man of letters to describe Liverpool. He wrote on the port in some detail in his "A Tour Through Great Britain":

The town was, at my first visiting it, about the year 1680, a large handsome, well-built, and encreasing or thriving town; at my second visit, anno 1690, it was much bigger than at my first seeing it ... but I may safely say that at this my third seeing of it . . . I was surpriz'd at the view, it was more than double what it was at the second . . . what it may grow to in time I know not...

The houses are exceedingly well-built, the streets straight, clean and spacious, and they are now well supplied with water. The merchants have a very pretty Exchange, standing upon 12 freestone columns, but it begins to be so much too little that it is thought they must remove or enlarge it.

Defoe records how he was ferried over the "Mersee" which at full sea, is more than two miles over."

We land on the flat shore on the other side, and are contented to ride through the water for some length, not on horseback, but on the shoulders of some honest Lancashire clown, who comes knee-deep to the boat-side, to truss you up, and then runs away with you as nimbly as you desire to ride, unless his trot were easier; for I was shaken by him that I had the luck to be carried by more

Daniel Defoe described Liverpool's Second Town Hall as 'a very pretty Exchange'. He also wrote 'Liverpool is one of the wonders of Britain'.

than I care for.

Liverpool is one of the wonders of Britain. In a word, there is no town in England, London excepted, that can equal Liverpool for the fineness of the streets and the beauty of the building.

There is a reference in one of the letters in the Picton Library to one of Defoe's visits. Sir Thomas Johnson (after whom modern Sir Thomas Street is named) wrote in 1705: "We have had Mr. Defoe here, I did not see him."

Sir Thomas did not approve of Defoe being entertained in Liverpool, for Johnson was at that time engaged in defrauding the Customs and knew that Defoe sometimes acted as a political spy. Johnson had good reason not to encourage eminent visitors. A year later a pamphlet appeared entitled: "A Trip to Leverpoole. A Satyre address'd to the Honourable the Commissioners of Her Majesties Customs." In this, references are made to the defrauding of the Customs as the reason why Liverpool had become so great:

> *So wealthy grown, so full of hurry,*
> *That she eclipses Bristol's Glory:*
> *Her Trade, as well as Sumptuous Houses,*
> *Where the Chief Publican carouses,*
> *In modern England called Collector,*
> *Does Manifestly Testify,*
> *Her Mightiness a Mystery*

Already the literary image of Liverpool was an amalgamation of the very good and the very bad. Unfortunately Liverpool did not produce essayists comparable with Defoe, who made much of his reputation as a journalist. An early attempt was made to establish a newspaper in Liverpool, the *Leverpool Courant* (1712) which might have encouraged local writers as later newspapers have done. Only a few issues appeared, of which no copies have survived, but it is known that the issue of July 15, 1712, consisted of London political news and some advertisements. The town was not yet rich enough or large enough to support a local newspaper.

The building of Liverpool's first dock in 1715 and the success of Liverpool's privateers in the war of the Austrian Succession 1739-48 created the wealth not only for building the present town hall, designed by John Wood of Bath, and opened in 1754, but also to support the first successful newspaper – *Williamson's Liverpool Advertiser and Mercantile Register,* which commenced publication in 1756.

Williamson had earlier published a year book in 1752, which reported that trade had spread her golden wings for Liverpool during the War of the Austrian Succession and that her privateers had been most successful. One of these – Fortunatus Wright – had almost incredible successes in the Mediterranean, became a national figure, and did much to create the literary image of Liverpool as a home of tough, ruthless seafarers. Another privateer who served with Wright was William Hutchinson. He later became dockmaster at Liverpool and wrote the first Liverpool practical manual of seamanship, which ran through several editions and gave many hints on how to become a successful privateer.

The first number of *Williamson's Advertiser* contained an announcement of the outbreak of the Seven Years' War, 1756-63, which involved war with France, as did also the War of American Independence, 1775-82.

A remarkable biography of John Coleman, a Liverpool baker who invested in privateering, has just been discovered by Mrs. D. Jacob, who is editing it for publication. It has recently been deposited in the Record Office of the Picton Library by its owner. Though quite brief, this autobiography reveals that its author had an excellent command of prose, although he left school at the age of seven. It shows how strong the Puritan tradition was in Liverpool – Coleman's Sundays were extremely strict. He worked hard to maintain his brothers and sisters on the death of his father, made a fortune, and secured a contract for supplying the French prisoners of war with bread. He was also encouraged to invest in privateering which brought on his bankruptcy. .

His autobiography ought to be published in book form, if only to modify the literary image that Liverpool shipowners were remorseless privateers and slave traders.

During the 18th century Liverpool's pottery industry thrived. Teapots, jugs and similar ware were inscribed with verses which were probably composed locally and gave some idea of the literary taste of the day. One described what a sailor found on his return from the wars:

> *Now safe from all alarms*
> *I rushed and found my Friend and Wife*
> *Locked in each others Arms.*
> *Yet fancy not*
> *I bore my lot*
> *Tame like a lubber — No*
> *For seeing I was finely tricked*
> *Plump to the devil I boldly Kick'd*
> *My Poll and Partner Joe.*

A six gallon jug with an illustration depicting fortune telling from coffee grounds read:

> *Here's luck in the bottom dear Jane only see,*
> *My dream and my Coffee in a Wedding agree,*
> *But ah! my dear sister what fate me befall,*
> *I fear I can wait for no wedding at all.*

It is interesting to note that the success of Liverpool's pottery industry was due to the invention of the art of transfer printing on pottery by a Liverpool man — John Sadler, who started business as a printer in 1748. He took out a patent in 1756. Printing on pottery coincided approximately with the establishment of the first successful newspaper in Liverpool and served also to encourage literacy.

The account book of Arthur Heywood, another merchant, who was associated with privateering and founded Heywood's Bank, reveals that he spent considerable sums on the purchase of books, so that the audience was being created for Liverpool to support her own creative writers.

About this time a subscription library was founded (c. 1756) by a conversation club which used to meet in the home of William Everard, schoolmaster. The books were kept at first in Everard's parlour and in 1758 they were moved to a separate establishment. The first catalogue of 1758 listed 177 works and 48 pamphlets in 450 volumes. There were 109 subscribers at an annual subscription of 5s. In 1760 the catalogue listed 150 volumes, in 1770, 1,547. Everard was appointed secretary and librarian in 1769, but was removed from office in 1770. After a number of moves the library was eventually established in the Lyceum in Bold Street.

Liverpool was clearly becoming a literary centre. Further

The Lyceum *(From an engraving by G. and C. Pyne)*

The enlarged Theatre Royal *(From an engraving by G. and C. Pyne)*

evidence was the increased publication of books in Liverpool. The earliest known book printed in Liverpool was "Hymns Sacred to the Lord's Table," printed by S. Terry in 1712. Terry also printed a sermon on the death of Queen Anne, and several other sermons, including one on the promotion of a charity school in Liverpool.

Adam Sadler carried on Terry's work, breaking new ground with "The Lawyer or Compleat Knave" (1728), Seacombe's "Memoirs of the House of Stanley" (1741), "The Muses' Delight" (1747) and a number of Catholic publications. Williamson printed Dr. Ibbetson's "Liverpool Spa Water." John Gore published the first Liverpool directory in 1766 and established the first well-known bookshop. He also published a newspaper, *Gore's Advertiser*.

Some of the important works on Liverpool were published outside the town, including the first history of Liverpool by Dr. Enfield which was printed in Warrington in 1773. Hodgson, of Pool Lane, Liverpool, published some poetry, including "Wrongs of Almoonar or the African's Revenge," and Peter Newby's "Poems" (1790). Another important influence in encouraging literature was the theatre, Nicholas Blundell, squire of Crosby Hall, recorded that he visited Liverpool in 1704; "My wife and I went to Leverpool and saw acted The Earl of Essex." In 1712 he recorded: "went to Leverp. and saw acted in ye Castle the Play called Yeoman of Kent."

The Drury Lane theatre was opened in 1759 and was visited by Samuel Derrick, Master of Ceremonies at Bath, the arbiter of 18th century taste. He wrote: "the scenes are perfectly painted. They play three times a week, and behind the boxes there is a table spread, in the manner of a coffee house, with tea, coffee, wine, cakes, fruit and punch."

The Theatre Royal was opened in 1772. Here Mrs. Siddons played Hamlet: "I played Hamlet in Liverpool to nearly a hundred pounds." One of Liverpool's actresses, Elizabeth Farren, became Lord Derby's second wife. Lord Derby was an enthusiastic amateur actor and patron of literature. The Theatre Royal would not put on any but London performances for many, years. When, on one occasion provincials appeared, the audience "threw up their hats, hissed, kicked, stamped, bawled . . . and saluted with volleys of potatoes and broken bottles."

Clearly there was a taste for the best in drama, and the background was appropriate for the emergence of a group of Liverpool writers of some distinction.

Liverpool Sailor, 1750
*"To see so many rough hewn Faces,
The Saylor's Hitch in all their Paces"*

Chapter 4

Later Hanoverian Writing (1): William Roscoe; James Currie; Slaver Hugh Crow; Explorer John Bradbury, Washington Irving.

By the time of the outbreak of the War of American Independence in 1775, circumstances in Liverpool were favourable for the production of a writer of some rank. There was, in Liverpool the Lyceum Library, Gore's bookshop, several newspapers and the new Theatre Royal, while in the commercial field several banks had been established, including Heywood's, as well as Liverpool's first insurance company, while the dock system had been considerably enlarged.

Civic pride in Liverpool's achievements was the motive which activated the first writings of William Roscoe. Liverpool's increased importance explains why the *Gentlemen's Magazine* was anxious to publish contributions from Roscoe. By origin, Roscoe was a poor boy. He helped his father in his market garden and to convey potatoes to market, before entering Gore's bookshop. Later, he was apprenticed as an attorney, but he was largely self-educated. As quite a young boy he copied out selections from Shenstone, Pope and other poets into manuscript books, written and laid out elegantly and with illustrations. He made a number of these before his first published work appeared. This was a poem called "Mount Pleasant," which was well-reviewed, although it is imitative and can hardly be claimed as poetry. It is, however, notable for its pride in Liverpool.

The early manuscript version was inscribed to his first love, Marian Done, to whom he wrote love poems. At the head of manuscript version he sketched a view of Liverpool as seen from the rural retreat at the top of Mount Pleasant. This was then in the country which extended for miles behind the site of the modern Adelphi Hotel. From the top of Mount Pleasant could be seen the hills of Wales which appear in the sketch and a panoramic view of Liverpool's spire. This view confirm's Wesley's, Defoe's and Celia Fienne's description of the old borough as a very pleasant, neat town.

Liverpool was for many years a holiday resort, in which a summer season of plays was acted by players from Drury Lane Theatre in London.

'Mount Pleasant' begins:

> *Eased of the cares that daily throng my breast,*
> *Again beneath my native shades, I rest.*
> *These native shades were oft I wont to stray,*
> *Ere fancy bow'd of reasons boasted sway.*

Roscoe's pride and love of Liverpool is expressed in glowing terms:

> *Now o'er the wondering world her name resounds*
> *From Northern climes, to India's distant bounds,*
> *Where e're his shores the broad Atlantic laves;*
> *Where e're the Baltic rolls his wintry waves . . .*
> *Her name in time's perennial list enroll'd*
> *Shall rank with those which Commerce lov'd of old;*
> *And teach mankind, how vain the pride that springs*
> *From the short glory of terrestial things.*

This type of poetry has now gone out of fashion. In the early 18th century, poetry was expected to be philosophic and to express, as Pope put it, "what oft was thought, but ne're so well expressed."

In choosing to write this type of poetry, and in using the highly Latinised polite vocabulary of the day, Roscoe turned his back on the vivid Northern idioms which were at hand. Liverpool, through its amalgam of English, Scots, Welsh and Irish, was already being distinguished by a quickness of wit which was later to produce an unparalleled list of comedians and actors.

Shakespeare did not disdain to use the vivid homely language of the people as a contrast to the stately language of the great, and Roscoe, too, recognised the earthy genius of Robert Burns, whom he assisted in several ways. But Roscoe did not follow the way Burns trod and his poetry cannot be

William Roscoe
(From the painting by Sir Martin Archer Shee in the Walker Art Gallery, Liverpool)

MOUNT PLEASANT

A POEM

inscribed to MARIA.

by W. Roscoe.

Eas'd of the cares that daily throng my breast,
Again beneath my native shades I rest;
These native shades, where oft I won't to stray
Ere fancy bow'd to reasons boasted sway.

Manuscript of William Roscoe
(Picton Reference Library, Liverpool)

ranked highly. The opinions Roscoe expressed in his poems were more original. As a Reformer, he believed in political and religious liberty and welcomed the outbreak of the French Revolution with a song which was very successful and appeared in many editions:

O'er the vine-covered hills and gay regions of France,
See the day star of liberty rise
Through the clouds of detraction unwearied advance
And hold its new course through the skies.

In "Mount Pleasant" Roscoe attacked the slave trade, and followed this up with two poetic volumes "The Wrongs of Africa."

Later in 1807, during his brief period as Member of Parliament for Liverpool, he voted for the abolition of the slave trade, and continued for another 20 years to press for its abolition through the world. He stuck to his beliefs when Pitt's Combination Act compelled him to disband the informal meetings he used to hold with his fellow Reformers in Liverpool, to discuss not only political but also literary and cultural questions. One of his reforming friends was James Currie, who also took part in the campaign for the abolition of the slave trade, and who wrote the first life story of Burns. Currie was joint author with Roscoe of "The African" which attacked the slave trade.

As a member of the licensing board for ships' doctors in the slave trade, he had much inside knowledge. In opposing the slave trade, Roscoe was following the tradition set in Liverpool by most of her authors. Thomas Lurting narrated in his 17th century autobiography how he refused to sell his Turkish captors into slavery and landed them with peaceful embraces, although they had intended to sell him as a slave. John Newton, who was, for a number of years a tide waiter in Liverpool and was active in the slave trade, repented later and became an opponent of the trade.

Unfortunately, the literary image which Liverpool's writers were creating of a city opposed to the slave trade was never very popular. Broad sections of the public wanted Liverpool to be portrayed as a city of vice, which is its fate in television plays today.

Dr. James Currie, author of the first biography of Robert Burns.
(From an engraving by J. Williamson)

The Athenaeum *(From an engraving by T. Troughton)*

Captain Hugh Crow, Liverpool Slave Captain, author of a vivid autobiography.

There was vice enough in 18th century Liverpool to justify this, but the critics of Liverpool were not content with this; they invented imaginary vice, affirming that slaves were bought and sold in large numbers in Liverpool itself. The truth is that slaves did not come to Liverpool in large numbers and Liverpool was the last of the great European ports to enter the slave trade. She undercut all other ports of Spain, Portugal, England, etc. because of her favourable economic position to develop the triangular run from Liverpool to Africa with industrial goods, from Africa to the New World with slaves, bought in the main from their compatriots, then back from the New World to Liverpool with sugar, rum, etc.

A well known Liverpool slave captain — Hugh Crow — described in his autobiography the harsh treatment he received as a prisoner of war and complained that no one was prepared to write in his support. He affirmed also that the conditions of the slaves in his ships were better than they received at home. Crow took the last slave ship out of Liverpool in 1807.

If Roscoe was not successful in creating a favourable literary image of Liverpool in Great Britain, he was successful abroad. As a prison reformer, and as a supporter of the Botanical Expedition of John Bradbury up the Missouri in 1812, and as a correspondent and friend of the American naturalist, Audobon, he achieved a great reputation in the United States. An extract from one of his letters to Jefferson on liberty was inscribed on the stones of the American Memorial Library in Berlin shortly after the end of the Second World War.

As a botanist, Roscoe's chief work is "Monandrian Plants" which is a collectors' piece and probably the most beautiful piece of printing ever done in Liverpool. Many of the original coloured drawings and manuscripts of this work came up for sale at Sotheby's and were acquired for the City. As a collector of pictures, drawings and prints, Roscoe was among the most far-seeing men of his age, and the Roscoe collection in the Walker Art Gallery is the kernel of its greatness. Roscoe's collection of books was equally great, if not greater, for books were his first and main love. His pictures and prints were bought as much to illustrate his Italian studies as *per se.* Unfortunately, his library was substantially dispersed and the Picton Library and the Athenaeum have only a small selection.

Roscoe's best-known and most frequently anthologised poem was on parting with his books, when he failed as a banker:

As one who destined from his friends to part,
Regrets his loss, yet hopes again erstwhile
To share their converse and enjoy their smile,
And tempers as he may Afflictions dart.

Roscoe's Italian studies and his biographies were translated into several European languages, and he achieved a wide reputation in Italy and France. The earliest printed book in the Picton Library — a very rare and beautiful edition of Petrarch — was presented to him by an Italian admirer after hearing of his bankruptcy.

Because Roscoe loved books so much, he took a prominent part in the establishment of the Athenaeum Library. He was also closely associated with the Literary and Philosophical Society, which was founded in 1812, and of which he was president for many years. Washington Irving has described in memorable terms his visit to Liverpool and the veneration he felt on meeting Roscoe in the Athenaeum Library. Since Roscoe's death, a constant stream of American and other scholars have undertaken research on his achievements. From the point of Liverpool, his greatest achievement is that, more than any other man, he has helped to create the image of Liverpool as a city with claims to be considered one of the greatest provincial cultural centres in Great Britain.

The Butterfly's Ball (1806) was the first children's book ever to be published. It became a nursery classic, and George III had it set to music for his children.

Chapter 5

Later Hanoverian Writing (2): General Tarleton;
the Richmonds; Felicia Hemans; De Quincey.

5

Contemporary with Roscoe were a number of writers with associations with Liverpool who achieved in some cases an international reputation outside the reforming field in which Roscoe and his friends made their mark.

One of Roscoe's contemporaries and his political opponent was Colonel Banastre Tarleton, who achieved fame as a cavalry leader during the War of American Independence. Tarleton wrote a number of letters on the campaign which have survived. Photostats of the originals are in the Picton Library. He had his portrait painted by Sir Joshua Reynolds, which was exhibited at one of the early art exhibitions with which Roscoe was associated. Tarleton also wrote a considerable volume on the American campaign which was the first military study of any size to be produced by a Liverpool writer. The first edition of this work was acquired at Sotheby's for the Picton Library.

Tarleton was a Tory, while Roscoe was a Whig. Feelings ran high in elections in those days, and both sides issued many political squibs which give some idea of the literary taste of the day. The poet laureate of the Liverpool Tories was Silvester Richmond, a great wit, who was searcher of customs at Liverpool and achieved a reputation for his squibs. His relative, the Rev. Legh Richmond, achieved a wide reputation in a different sphere.

Legh Richmond was born in Liverpool in 1772. He became a best seller with his novelettes, "The Dairyman's Daughter" and "The Young Cottager." "The Dairyman's Daughter" has been claimed to have been read by more people in proportto the population of the day than any novel ever

Colonel Banastre Tarleton
(From the painting by Sir Joshua Reynolds in the National Gallery)

written. It drips with a pious unctuosity which the age admired but which does not attract readers to-day.

Another writer who has substantially lost popularity is Felicia Hemans, who was born in Liverpool at 118 Duke Street, which still stands to-day and bears a plaque commemorating her birth. Felicia Dorothea Hemans nee Browne, was born in 1793, when the outbreak of war with France brought ruin to many merchants. Credit was at a standstill and was only revived when the Corporation obtained power by Act of Parliament to issue bank notes on its own credit. This was to provide the means for re-establishing confidence which had been destroyed by the failure of a number of banks, as a result of which their bank notes were valueless. Felicia Hemans' father survived this crisis, but failed five years later following the financial panic caused by the landing of French troops in Cardigan Bay in 1797.

After the bankruptcy of her father, Mrs. Hemans lived in various places, mainly in Wales, and received encouragement from William Roscoe. She corresponded with Shelley, but her mother cut this short. Her first volume of poems was written between the age of eight and thirteen and she became known as the English Sappho. She published three volumes of poems between 1808 and 1812, when she married a Captain Hemans from North Wales.

In 1818 her husband left her and she wrote many works to earn her living, including "Songs Of Affections," "The Siege of Valencia" and "Records of Women."

In 1827 she came to live in High Street, Wavertree, where she remained until 1831. Her reputation was so high that her house was visited by many noted people and autograph hunters. In particular she attracted American visitors, who used to carry away as souvenirs such mundane objects as pebbles from her path or a spray from her trees in her garden. Her American reputation was due mainly to her well-known poem "The Landing of the Pilgrim Fathers." Mrs. Heman's best known poem in England is "Casabianca." Casabianca was the 13-years-old son of The Admiral of the Orient, in the Battle of the Nile. All the crew was killed with the exception of Casabianca, who remained at his post on the burning deck, not knowing that his father was lying dead below.

The boy stood on the burning deck,

Felicia Hemans

> *whence all but he had fled,*
> *The flame that lit the battle's work*
> *shone round him o're the dead.*

After her death, at the early age of 41, William Wordsworth referred to her as "that holy spirit, sweet as the spring, as ocean deep." While living at Wavertree, Mrs. Hemans visited the local academy, which she celebrated in the poem, "On visiting a girls' school at the hour of evening prayer." The Picton Library possesses a number of her manuscripts, including that of "The Forest Sanctuary."

Unlike Roscoe, Mrs. Hemans was not a local patriot; she disliked Liverpool and its residents and longed to return to her hills in Wales, referring to Liverpool's "waveless horizon! how it wearies the eyes . . . it is a dull uninventive nature all around here, though there must be somewhere little fairy nooks, which I hope by degrees to discover." Of the local society, she wrote that it was "exclusively under the dominion of an aristocracy of wealth."

Another woman writer of this period having associations with Liverpool was Mrs. Sherwood, who wrote a number of popular romances characterised by sentiment which differed only in degree, but not in kind from that which made the works of Legh Richmond and Mrs. Hemans so popular. In one of her novels she describes her arrival in Liverpool on the Kingsmill, owned by Sir John Gladstone, father of the Prime Minister. This was the first ship to arrive in Liverpool from India, after the partial abolition of the East India Company's monopoly of trade in 1813, when Liverpool's merchants were at long last permitted to trade with the East. Mrs. Sherwood describes the large crowd which greeted the arrival of the ship and the service held in St. Nicholas's Church.

Some other well-known writers were severely critical of Liverpool. De Quincey stayed for a period in a cottage at Everton and was entertained by the banker Clarke, and dined with Roscoe and the Rev. William Shepherd, the literary parson from Gateacre. De Quincey severely criticised the Liverpool literary coterie in his "Confessions of an English Opium Eater," over 30 years after his visit, and drew a vigorous reply from Shepherd, the only Liverpool survivor of the group.

God Save the Poor.

A Song published by Mr. Chalmer, of Liverpool, on the Notice for allowing the Irish Distilleries to work, which immediately raised Corn in Ireland 40 per Cent, and on the Proposal in Parliament for allowing the British Distilleries to work, which instantly raised Wheat 2s. 6d. and Potatoes 1s. per Bushel through-out the North.

LANCASHIRE had Bread enough,
  Till Jenkinson came there;
They never had a decent Loaf,
  Since He did interfere.

CHORUS.
The brave, the loyal Lancashire,
  They for their King will fight,
The Poor have said, We have no Bread,
  Ye noble Lords do right;
The Poor do cry, our Wants supply,
  Ye noble Lords do right,

SONG---*AFFETTUOSO*.

GOD save the wretched Poor,
  God save the afflicted Poor,
      God save the Poor.
They sweat and toil all Day,
Taxes and Rates to pay,
  Yet cannot clear their Way,
      God save the Poor.

All through the War the Poor,
Mighty Griefs did endure,
      God save the Poor.
Great Men did trade in Corn,
Which made the Poor forlorn,
Poor folks were overborne.
      God save the Poor.

Much Gain by Corn they Made,
This made them love the Trade,
      God save the Poor.
This made them still go on,
Till the Poor were undone,
And Comfort they had none,
      God save the Poor.

———————

Printed at the Anti-Starvation Office, Kent Street, Liverpool, by

Francis Chalmer, Grand Anti-starvator.

Song on bread shortage – 1801

De Quincey described how Roscoe strongly criticised the Scottish aristocracy for its shabby treatment of Burns. This part of his account is true, for a letter in the Roscoe Papers in the Picton Library confirms this. De Quincey had no criticism of Everton as a place of residence, for he found peace there after running away from Manchester Grammar School, referring to Liverpool as a Hyperion to a Satyr. The friendly rivalry between Manchester and Liverpool existed during this period, as it does now. The "men" of Manchester resented the cultural pretensions of the "gentlemen" of Liverpool. In 1825 the following song was sung at the Theatre Royal, Manchester, which welcomed the proposal to bring Liverpool down a peg by building a ship canal from Manchester to Parkgate and so avoid paying ship dues to Liverpool:

Alas then for poor Liverpool, she'd surely go to pot Sir,
For want of trade her folks would starve, her Custom
  House would rot, Sir,
I'm wrong, they'd not exactly starve or want,
  for it is true, Sir,
They might come down to Manchester, and we could
  find them work to do, Sir.

The belief in Manchester that Liverpool was a rich town, where people did not work, was understandably not shared by the poor of Liverpool.

Francis Chalmers, writing from the Anti-Starvation Office, Kent Street, Liverpool, chose to describe the misery caused by the shortage of bread in the following poetic terms:

God save the Poor,
They sweat and toil all Day,
Taxes and Rates to pay,
Yet cannot clear their way ...
All through the War the Poor
Mighty griefs did endure ...
Great Men did trade in corn,
Which made the Poor forlorn ...

This is not great poetry but already the sorrows of the poor in Liverpool were finding some literary expression. Roscoe and some other writers of the period 1775-1831 were concerned with broad ideals, which led to reform. It was not until the early Victorian age that the social problems of Liverpool found expression in the writings of Dickens and other writers.

De Quincey's cottage at Everton

Chapter 6

Early Victorian Writing from Liverpool: Arthur Hugh Clough;
the Brontës; Charles Dickens; Melville; Hawthorne; Carlyle;
Lear.

The enormous growth of Liverpool in the early 19th century was in part due to the development of overseas trade and the complete abolition in 1833 of the East India Company's monopoly of trade with the East. This gave new opportunities to Liverpool's merchants and attracted new-comers from all parts of the world. But it was the famine in Ireland which caused an exceptional rush from Ireland, over 200,000 landing in Liverpool in a single year, thus aggravating the slum problem. In addition Liverpool was struck by a succession of cholera epidemics.

Against this background, it is not surprising that the literary image of Liverpool in early Victorian literature is grim. The literary image in the 18th century had reflected privateering and the slave trade, which had come to an end. These had not lacked some colour and romance, which it was hard to find in the unrelieved misery of the Liverpool poor, to which many prominent writers referred — Dickens, the Brontes, etc.

Surprisingly, the only poet of distinction of Liverpool origin during this period was philosophical and did not concern himself excessively with the social conditions in his poems — Arthur Hugh Clough. His sister, on the contrary, was one of the prominent social reformers who collectively made Liverpool the pioneer of the Welfare state in the early Victorian period — in public health, baths, libraries, etc. Arthur Hugh Clough was born in Rodney Street, Liverpool, in 1819, and was the son of a cotton merchant. Shortly after his birth, his family moved to the United States, but Clough was educated in England at Rugby. In 1836 his parents returned to Liverpool. In 1837 he went to Oxford, becoming later principal of University Hall, University College, London. He married and lived an uneventful life until his death in 1861. At intervals during his life he published poems, and became a close friend of Matthew Arnold whose well-known poem "Thyrsis" lamented Clough's death. Both Arnold and Clough were products of the Arnold regime at Rugby and aspired to a self-consciously spiritual standard of life, which the modern age, with its rejection of so many Victorian standards, tends to regard as priggish. During the second world war, Winston Churchill quoted in one of his broadcasts from one of Clough's poems, which is representative of his concern with the mysteries of life and death and his inward struggle to snatch some hope from despair.

Say not the struggle nought availeth,
The labour and the wounds are vain,
The enemy faints not, nor faileth,
And as things have been they remain.

The verse quoted by Winston Churchill symbolised his hope even in the darkest days of the Second World War.

And not by Eastern windows only,
When daylight comes, comes in the light.
In front, the sun climbs slow, how slowly.
But westward, look, the land is bright.

Whereas Clough drew a qualified hope from the despair of life, his contemporary Bramwell Bronte gave way to morbidity. He stayed in Liverpool much longer than he intended in 1839 and after paying off "several debts of which my father or aunt had no knowledge," was in great poverty. He was again in Liverpool in 1845: "Wherever I went a certain woman robed in black, and calling herself Misery walked by my side." In 1839, Charlotte Bronte wrote: "Aunt and Papa have determined to go to Liverpool for a fortnight and to take us all with them." Because the Brontes knew Liverpool and its misery well, it is not surprising that Heathcliff, the villain of Emily Bronte's "Wuthering Heights" was a Liverpool gypsy stray picked up by Mr. Earnshaw in the streets of Liverpool.

Dickens also paid his first visit to Liverpool in the early years of Queen Victoria's reign. In 1838 he met his eventual biographer, John Forster, by arrangement at the Adelphi Hotel. He had just completed "Oliver Twist," so that his interest in social questions had already expressed itself powerfully in a novel before he came to Liverpool. In 1842, Dickens made another visit to Liverpool, prior to sailing with his wife in the Cunarder Britannia, which had inaugurated the first, regular cross-Atlantic steamship service from Liverpool in 1840. In his "American Notes," Dickens describes the Britannia and the trials of the passengers whilst crossing the Atlantic.

In 1844, Dickens was back in Liverpool to take the chair at a soirée at the Mechanics Institute, Mount Street. In 1847 he acted the part of Captain Bobadil in Ben Johnson's "Every Man His Humour" at the Theatre Royal for a benefit for Leigh Hunt. The next year he appeared in "The Merry Wives of Windsor" in aid of a permanent curatorship for Shakespeare's house in Stratford and in 1852 appeared at the Philharmonic Hall in Bulwer Lytton's play "Not So Bad As We Seem," which raised funds for the Guild of Literature and Art.

Dickens wrote to Lytton: "I left Liverpool at four o'clock in the morning, and I am so blinded by excitement, gas, waving hats and handkerchiefs that, believe me, I can hardly see to write, but nevertheless it was a night of triumph."

During his visits, Dickens visited the docks, talked to the sailors and gathered knowledge of social conditions, which he used in his novels, e.g. "The Uncommercial Traveller." Here he describes the vice and drunkenness of the sailors in the 1860's. He also made literary use of his visit to Liverpool Workhouse. In 1857, Dickens made his debut in Liverpool as a public reader of his own works. His last reading was in 1869 when the old Theatre Royal was renovated for this purpose. He was entertained at a banquet at St. George's Hall. After the toast to his health Dickens said that Liverpool had never failed him when he had asked for help for literature or benevolence. Writing from the Adelphi Hotel to his doctor, Dickens stated that "the last prescription goes against my

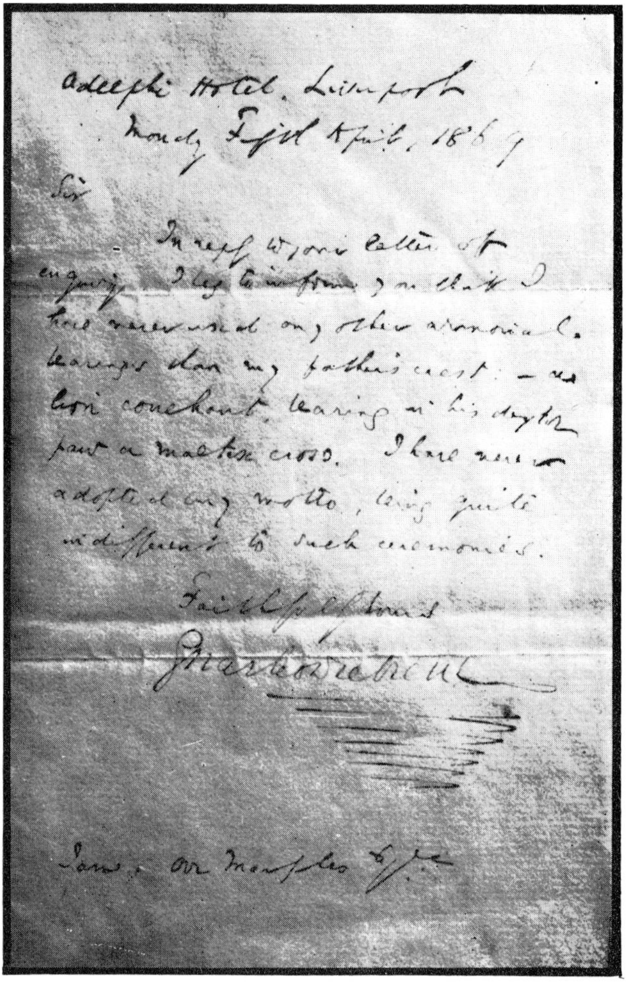
Adelphi Hotel, Liverpool
Monday Fifth April, 1869

Sir

In reply to your letter of enquiry, I beg to inform you that I have never used any other armorial bearings than my father's crest – a lion couchant, bearing in his dexter paw a Maltese cross. I have never adopted any motto, being quite indifferent to such ceremonies.

Faithfully yours
Charles Dickens

James Marples Esq.

Original Dickens letter from the Adelphi Hotel

... with an autographed portrait

stomach . . . if I were living another kind of life than a reading one, this might not be, but I am so easily nauseated after these nightly exercises that I sometimes in the morning cannot bear the taste in my mouth." In 1870 he died.

Two distinguished American visitors to early Victorian Liverpool referred in their works to the horrors of Liverpool's streets — Herman Melville and Nathaniel Hawthorne.

Herman Melville was born in New York in 1819 and ran away to sea as a boy before the mast in 1837 sailing first to Liverpool, which he described as "Redburn". Melville paid tribute to "the nobel spectacle of its great new granite docks, its rows and rows of gloomy warehouse, its handsome public buildings, The Town Hall and the Custom House, and the Lancashire countryside, still so richly English." This was the background to the "putridity, vice and crime which reeked up from among the pestilent alleys of Liverpool." Melville describes with Hogarthian detail a Spanish sailor's murder of a prostitute at a bar in Liverpool, the barbaric floggings on American vessels, and an epidemic in the steerage. Melville wrote: "Of all seaports in the world, Liverpool, perhaps, most abounds in all the varieties of land-sharks, land-rats and other vermin which makes the hapless mariner their prey." Yet Melville added that sailors loved Liverpool above all other ports.

Nathaniel Hawthorne served for four years as U.S. Consul in Liverpool from 1857 to 1861. He had an office near the Goree Piazza and a house at Rock Ferry overlooking the Mersey. On his appointment his wife wrote: "The office is second in dignity only to the Embassy in London, and is more sought for than any other, and is nearly the most lucrative." Hawthorne described how he disliked his duties in Liverpool in his English note books. Shortly after Hawthorne's arrival in Liverpool, the foundation stone was laid of the Brown Library, which was the first large, specially built public library in Great Britain. It was presented to the city by Sir William Brown, an American cotton merchant in Liverpool who founded the firm of Brown, Shipley and Company, now merchant bankers. Sir William Brown was also first chairman of the Bank of Liverpool.

In presenting the Brown Library to Liverpool, he made the study of literature possible for thousands of Liverpudlians

Said the Duck to the Kangaroo,
    "Good gracious! how you hop!
Over the fields and the water too —
    As if you never would stop!
My life is a bore in this nasty pond,
And I long to go out in the world beyond!
    I wish I could hop like you!"
    Said the Duck to the Kangaroo.

"Please give me a ride on your back!"
    Said the Duck to the Kangaroo,—
"I would sit quite still, and say nothing but 'Quack'
    The whole of the long day through!
And we'd go to the Dee, and the Jelly Bo Lee,
Over the land, and over the sea;—
    Please take me a ride—o do!"
    Said the Duck to the Kangaroo.

Manuscript of Edward Lear's *The Duck and the Kangaroo*

who would otherwise have not had access to books. Many of these became writers, some, like Hall Caine, of great reputation.

With the opening of the Brown Library in 1860, the early Victorian period in Liverpool may be considered to have come to an end with an achievement which did something to counteract the terrible image of Liverpool in the works of so many writers. Not all eminent Victorians failed to see something good in Liverpool. Thomas Carlyle visited Liverpool frequently with his wife. On his first visit he wrote: "I found time to be impressed by the seeming efficiency of the inhabitants; they appeared to me to be remarkably go-ahead people. Streets, streets, streets! Market places, churches, theatres, shops . . . I confess amazement at the preponderance of public houses . . . As I observed comparatively little insobriety, I considered that many of these places relied on foreign seamen for their trade . . . a gratifying thought because I rather like Liverpool and its people." Carlyle was very discerning and his remarks explain why Liverpool people continue to be amazed at the frequent literary presentation of Liverpool as the home of vice. This exists, no doubt, but much of it is unknown to the ordinary Liverpudlian for it is imported from outside.

Edward Lear worked at Knowsley Hall, Liverpool for four successive Earls of Derby, producing there his great children's classic the *Book of Nonsense*. A very early edition of this is in the Picton Library.

Thomas Greevey, the diarist was born in Wavertree.

Chapter 7

Mid-Victorian Writing from Liverpool: Sir James A. Picton; S.K. Hocking; Mrs. Oliphant; Matthew Arnold; W.E. Gladstone.

7

The mid-Victorian era in Liverpool's history may well be considered to have started with the American Civil War. During the war supplies of American cotton were cut off and there was much misery and unemployment in Lancashire.

The Liverpool blockade-runners did what they could to bring in supplies, and their exploits were colourful enough to inspire a contemporary work similar to, say, "The Cruel Sea," but they did not. During the war fortunes were made and lost in cotton on the Exchange Flags and were commemorated in some cotton rhymes:

> They bought themselves new traps and drags,
> They smoked the best cigars;
> And as they walked the Exchange Flags,
> They thanked their lucky stars.

At the end of the war bankruptcy came to many:

> Yes, Great King Cotton's been and gone,
> And cleaned his subjects out,
> And those who trusted him the most,
> Have vanished up the spout.

The financial crisis of 1866 hit Liverpool very hard, but it was only one of a succession of crises in the Victorian era which resulted in many bankruptcies.

Sir William Bower Forwood has described in his auto-biography the effect of this crisis and has done for merchant speculation what Hugh Crow did for the slave trade in his autobiography. Sir William's autobiography is important,

Sir William Bower Forwood

because he touched the life of Liverpool at so many points. He has left an account of his voyage to Australia on one of the legendary clippers of Liverpool of the day, whose captains and exploits were immortalised in contemporary sea-shanties. He was chairman for a period of the Bank of Liverpool and took a prominent part in the movement for the building of the Cathedral.

Another merchant whose writings illuminate the Victorian scene in Liverpool was George Melly, who issued a large number of pamphlets and books. Melly was also an explorer. The manuscript of his journey up the Nile is in the Picton Library, together with the collected edition of his published books, Press articles, etc. A cotton merchant of Swiss descent, Melly was a leader of the Liberal reformers who used to meet in the basement of the Royal Insurance Company, of which he was also, for a period, chairman.

Both Forwood and Melly came from a comfortable background of middle-class merchants. A greater literary figure of humbler origin was James Allanson Picton, after whom the Picton Library, Picton Road, and Picton Clock Tower, Wavertree, are named. As author of a number of historical volumes on Liverpool and of many papers, he permanently enriched local tradition. He served for over 40 years as chairman of the Libraries Committee, and if the mid-Victorian era had to be associated with the name of one person who served literature and learning in Liverpool, then it would be called the Age of Picton.

He was born in Liverpool in 1805. His father was a builder who was involved in financial difficulties and Picton had to leave school at the age of 13 to work in his father's timber yard.

Picton has left an authentic vivid account of the Liverpool of his youth: "Imagine a town of 100,000 inhabitants without gas, without railways, without steam-boats, without police . . . The streets were all paved with rough boulder stones . . . The miserable oil lamps at long distances apart, served only to make darkness visible . . . There were scavengers to sweep the streets. Their method was to sweep the mud into long parallelograms here and there about a foot deep, which were left for days . . . These heaps were called Corporation beds . . . I have known as many as ten stand-up fights after dark . . . outside our house."

James A. Picton

In 1821 Picton's father failed and he was put in the debtors' prison in Great Howard Street, where his son visited him. In 1825 their house was sold up over their heads, and they took refuge in an empty house. In 1826, Picton became assistant surveyor at 25s a week. In 1828 he married. On the death of his wife in 1879 Picton built Wavertree Clock Tower in her memory with the inscription "Time wasted is existence, used is life." It was quite common for the residents of Wavertree "to go and see the time by Sarah Picton."

Picton prospered as an architect, surveyor and valuer and retired at the age of 60 in 1866. He was able to devote the remainder of his life to literature, scholarship and public life. The Tower Buildings is his best known building still standing. In 1846 he joined the Literary and Philosophical Society to which he gave a number of papers. In 1849 he was one of the first members of the Historic Society of Lancashire and Cheshire. He was also an active member of the Philomathic Society. His finest literary works are his "Memorials of Liverpool," in two volumes, which took him seven years to compile. It remains a standard work and can never be superseded. His "Miscellaneous Essays and Addresses" are bound in a volume of some 500 pages and range over an astounding variety of subjects — Wren, William Cowper, the Liverpool Cathedral, Dialect, etc.

When the Picton Library was opened in 1879, Picton made some remarks which symbolise what he had done for Liverpool: "Look around on the vast array of books which crowd these shelves. They express the best thoughts of the noblest men of all ages and nations. They are the steps by which we rise from barbarism to civilisation, the aliment of mind, which is now so essential to modern society, that it is like the air we breathe." There is a stand in the centre of the Picton Library which is also emblematical. It was here that electric light was first displayed in any public building in Liverpool. As Picton put it: "May it be an emblem of the light of knowledge and truth which will be disseminated from this centre to quicken and vivify the minds of the population around." It is remarkable that Picton was able to achieve so much for libraries at a time when the pressure for housing and other public services was much greater than it is now. But he saw that it was precisely because t'   were under-

Chapter I

Brother and Sister

It was getting dark. Though the Town Hall clock had only just struck four. But a fog had hung all over Liverpool since morning, and everything was as damp and dismal as it well could be. and now as evening came on the fog had settled into a dense drizzle converting the streets into sluch seemed to Nelly Bates (who was crouched in the shadow of St. George's Church) endless puddles.

"Irish Benny would come" said she to herself "I wonder what has kept him. he said he be here, when the clock struck four."

And she wrapped her tattered clothes more closely around her, and looked eagerly down Lord Street and up and down Castle Street, but no Benny appeared in sight.

"I'm glad as how they's lighting the lamps anyhow. It'll make it feel a bit warmer I reckon" she went on "for its terrible cold. But Benny won't be long now: unless. Unless he's sold all his fusees"—

And she looked wistfully at the unsold matches lying in her lap. Then after a pause she went on again.

privileged that libraries were necessary.

The lives of the under-privileged in Liverpool continued to inspire literature during the mid-Victorian era. One of the best-known popular novels was "Her Benny" by Silas K. Hocking which was translated into many languages and sold hundreds of thousands of copies. Hocking held a pastorate at Grove Street, Liverpool, and the manuscript of "Her Benny", which is in the Picton Library, is written on official stationery.

It begins: "It was getting dark, though the Town Hall clock had only struck four. But a fog had hung all over Liverpool since morning and everything was as damp and dismal as it well could be; and now, as evening came on, the fog had settled into a downright drizzle, converting the streets into what seem to Nelly Bates (who was crouched in the shadow of St. George's Church) to be endless puddles. "I wish Benny would come," said she to herself, "I wonder what has kept him; he said he'd be here, when the clock struck four." And she wrapped her tattered clothes more closely around her, and looked eagerly down Lord Street and up and down Castle Street. But no Benny appeared in sight. "I'm glad as how they's lighting the lamps anyhow. It'll make it feel a bit warmer."

A woman writer who was moved to write as a result of her experiences in Liverpool was Mrs. M. Oliphant, who was born in Liverpool and was vividly impressed by the "great distress" among the people which was aggravated by wide scale immigration and cholera epidemics. When she was only 14, Mrs. Oliphant took an active part in the Anti-Corn Law movement in Liverpool. Her father acted as honorary treasurer of a relief fund and her brother distributed food. At the age of 16 she had her first romance at Everton. A year later she had another affair in Liverpool. During the long illness of her mother, whom she nursed, Mrs. Oliphant fell into the habit of writing in the intervals of bedside watching. After the publication of her first successful novel, "Margaret Maitland" (1849) her family went to live at Birkenhead the Carlingford of her novels, where she married her cousin in 1852. Between 1849 and 1897 she wrote well over 100 books. She was granted a civil pension.

The mid-Victorian era can perhaps appropriately be taken

as ending in 1888 — before the naughty nineties. It was in this year that Matthew Arnold died in Liverpool. His sister was a well-known local philanthropist, who was one of the original managers of Dingle Lane Council School, which was subsequently renamed Matthew Arnold Council School in his memory. Arnold had come to Liverpool to meet his daughter who was returning from New York. On the evening previous to his death he was in excellent spirits and attempted to jump a low fence. After luncheon on the following day he was walking down Dingle Lane when he suddenly dropped dead.

Augustine Bissell, the essayist, was born in School Lane, Liverpool.

Another famous Victorian to be associated with Liverpool was the Prime Minister, W.E.Gladstone, who wrote extensively. The original manuscript of his *Home Rule for Ireland* is in the Picton Library.

Original Cruikshank illustration for the first edition of Dickens's *Oliver Twist.*

Chapter 8

Late 19th Century and Early 20th Century:
Sir William Watson; Hall Caine; Richard Le Gallienne;
John Masefield.

In late Victorian and Edwardian England many of the institutions of modern Liverpool took their present form or were founded.

Liverpool became a city, the title of Lord Mayor was bestowed on her first citizen, the bishopric and university were founded, and the Pier Head trinity of buildings was erected. The size of the City was greatly extended by a succession of amalgamations. Liverpool produced or became associated with a considerable number of creative writers of great distinction. Not all these developments were approved.

Sir William Watson, for instance, wrote a poem criticising the decision to build the Cathedral while so many slums existed in Liverpool. Entitled "Thoughts on Revisiting a Centre of Commerce Where a Vast Cathedral Church is being Erected," it reads:

> *City of festering streets by Misery trod,*
> *Where half-fed, half clad children swarm unshod*
> *While thou dost rear that splendid fane to God.*
> *O rich in fruit and grains and oils and ores,*
> *And all things that the feastful Earth outpours,*
> *Yet lacking leechcraft for those leprous stores . . .*
> *Let nave and transept rest awhile; but when*
> *Thou hast done His work who lived and died for men,*
> *Then build His temple on high — not, not, till then.*

Sir William Watson was born in Yorkshire, but came to Liverpool at an early age with his father who was a merchant. For a period he resided in Salisbury Road, Cressington. Some of his early poems appeared in the *Liverpool Argus* in 1875, and his early volumes were published during his residence in Liverpool. His works include "The Prince's Quest" (1880), "Epigrams of Art, Life and Nature" (1883), "Wordsworth's Grave" (1890), "The Year of Shame" (1896), "For England" (1903). His last volume appeared in 1928. Although highly praised by Tennyson and immensely popular for a time — he was knighted in 1917 — his poetry is little read in the twentieth century. He was recommended for the poet laureateship, but was passed over.

In 1893 he received a Civil List pension, in the year that the title of Lord Mayor was bestowed on Liverpool's first citizen. Watson wrote the Anniversary Ode for Liverpool when she celebrated her 700th anniversary in 1907.

Deep in memory, deep in time;
Rooted far in England's prime,
Proud she stands among her peers,
Clothed with her seven hundred years.

In later years, Sir William felt estranged from Liverpool, and his widow would not allow his coffin to be conveyed through the streets when it was brought to Liverpool to be buried at Childwall.

Perhaps his best poetry was his poetic literary criticism of Wordsworth, Arnold and Shelley.

Fellow contributors with Watson to the *Liverpool Argus* were William Tirebuck, the novelist, who was commended by Tolstoy, and Hall Caine, whose novel "The Shadow of a Crime" was serialised in the *Liverpool Mercury*. Hall Caine, like Watson, was also knighted for services to Literature. Born at Runcorn, Hall Caine came to Liverpool at an early age and was educated in a school at Hope Street, which had been founded by the Unitarians. He started his career with a Welsh architect in Liverpool — Richard Owens "the Welshman who built more chapels in the northern counties of the Principality than all the other architects of his time put together." Caine once said: "I could sketch you one in a few minutes." Caine started his literary career writing for architectural and building papers and became a regular user of the Picton Library, which he called his university, and which possesses a considerable number of his manuscripts. He became leader writer of the *Liverpool Mercury,* which was later merged in the *Daily Post.* He moved to London, became secretary to Dante Gabriel Rosetti, who first encouraged him to write on the Isle of Man. In 1887 he became famous with "The Deemster". Many of his novels were filmed — "The Manxman", "The Eternal City", "The Prodigal Son", "The Woman Thou Gavest Me", "The Christian", etc.

His Liverpool contemporary, Fabian Lacon, recorded that "Tom" Caine became Hall Caine when he achieved success, and began to sport a Tennysonian cape. His son was for a period Member of Parliament for Liverpool, with which Hall Caine continued to maintain a close association.

Another late Victorian writer of distinction with Liverpool associations was Richard Le Gallienne, whose grandfather was a French sea captain who commanded his own ship — the Lucretia — between Liverpool, Panama and the West Indies. Le Gallienne's father was born in Everton, ran away from home at the age of 12, and obtained a post in the Water Street office of the Birkenhead Brewery Company, of which he became secretary. He left a fortune of over £30,000 on his death. Le Gallienne relied on his father's financial assistance during much of his life.

Le Gallienne served accountancy articles with Chalmers, Wade and Company in Fenwick Street, but gave this up for literature. To the youth of the nineties he made a great appeal and he was a friend of Oscar Wilde. Le Gallienne became a symbol of Romance, with his dusky curls and elegant cloak. His poem, "The Quest of the Golden Girl," achieved great success. It described the search of a modern troubadour for the ideal bride:

> *Her tears are in the falling rain*
> *She calls me in the wind's soft song,*
> *And with the flowers she comes again.*

A considerable volume of Le Gallienne's manuscripts were deposited in the Picton Library some time ago:

> *Strange craft of words, strange magic of the pen,*
> *Whereby the dead still talk with living men.*

Le Gallienne rode about the Cheshire countryside on one

Poet Laureate John Masefield on a visit to Liverpool College in **1930**
(Photo by courtesy of Liverpool Daily Post & Echo Ltd.)

of the penny farthings of the day. He wrote "Travels in England," based on his experiences as a cyclist, with a straw boater perched on his dark curls. This helped to build up his reputation as a dandy: "All my life," he told a reporter, "I have been endeavouring to live down the report that I wear silk bloomers."

The excellent recent life of Le Gallienne by two Liverpool authors – Richard Whittington-Egan and Geoffrey Smerdon – was published appropriately under the title "The Quest of the Golden Boy."

It was in the nineties that John Masefield first came to Liverpool, where he was a cadet on the old H.M.S. Conway, 1891-4, gaining prizes. Nevertheless, he was, owing to illness, prevented from following a life at sea. He made only one voyage in the sailing ships which he immortalised in his verse. It was in "the finest ship my eyes have ever seen" – the Wanderer. When he qualified as a merchant officer he was appointed sixth officer on the White Star Line's Adriatic, which he was to join in New York. But on arrival he gave up the sea and became alternately American barman, a hobo, a worker in a carpet factory and touched life at many points before he became a writer.

Masefield is undoubtedly best known in Liverpool as a poet of the sea. He wrote the history of H.M.S. Conway in two volumes, and has probably written more poems to commemorate events on Merseyside than any other poet. He wrote a prologue for the opening of the Liverpool Playhouse in 1911 and also to celebrate its 50th anniversary. He also wrote some lines for the Commonwealth regime at the Playhouse during the first world war. He wrote a Coronation poem for the city, and poems for Liverpool Cathedral of which he was appointed Counsellor. He commemorated in verse the visit to the Cathedral of the Queen and the Duke of Edinburgh. In agreeing to do this he stated: "I have always loved the great city of Liverpool. I have known it since 1891, loved it very much and have very happy memories of my days there."

Although Masefield was not born in Liverpool and did not often visit it, he is regarded by many as the poet of Liverpool, and it is a sign of Liverpool's emergence as a great city that it should have been so closely associated with him. Of Liverpool.

Masefield wrote:

You stand upon the highway of the sea
Wherein your ships, your children, come and go
In splendour at the full of every flow,
Bound to and from whatever ports may be.

Sketch of *Wanderer* — the subject of Masefield's
famous poem.

Chapter 9

The 20th Century (1): James Hanley; John Brophy;
John Owen; Arthur Behrend; Sir Hugh Walpole;
Marguerite Steen; Holbrook Jackson; Colin Brooks;
James Laver; John Pride.

In the 20th century the predominant literary image of Liverpool continued to be marked by a squalor which the two world wars merely intensified. But the spread of education and improved standards of living increased the number of potential readers and gave new opportunities for writing to persons who in the past could never have arisen above their circumstances.

For the first time in Liverpool's history there emerged in the period between the two world wars a novelist of great power who came from the under-privileged — James Hanley. He joined the Army at a very early age, serving with the First Canadians in the trenches, on transports at the Dardanelles and in the Mediterranean. Later he worked as dock labourer and railway porter. His vision of life is austere, tragic and original and his style rough and expressive. In order to be realistic he uses the language of the docker and the labourer.

Although he lived for many years in Wales, he has remained remarkably faithful to the sea and Liverpool as the background for his novels. The themes are everyday, and he develops them starkly. "The Last Voyage" is a terribly grim account of an old Liverpool fireman who has been told he cannot go to sea again. "Men in Darkness" is a collection of short stories, in which no lightness or happiness is allowed to enliven the lives of his Liverpool firemen and their women, whose main preoccupations are drinking, quarrelling or worrying over the possible loss of their jobs. "Ebb and Flood" is a powerful tale of an adolescent boiler scaler who alternately loves and curses his mute mother.

The four volumes of his Fury's Chronicle is the stark story

of an Irish family in Gelton. In a later novel he used the name Garlton. Both represent a fictional Liverpool. In some of his later novels Hanley takes the North country rather than Liverpool as a background, or even Wales in which he has so long lived, but he comes back to the tragic vision of Liverpool's dockland. In his later experiments with plays he is still obsessed with a view of damnation and despair.

The Picton Library possesses a considerable number of the original manuscripts of Hanley's works, which are neatly written in exercise books.

A writer with a background similar in some respects to that of Hanley is John Brophy. Like Hanley, Brophy served in the first world war at a very early age and chose Liverpool as the background for some of his novels. But Brophy came from a more literate background. He was educated at the Holt School and at Liverpool University. The Liverpool in his novels is sordid, but is not so starkly tragic as Hanley's. Many of his novels were filmed and were best sellers. In the "Rock Road" the background is Hammersands, a fictional Liverpool. "Waterfront" is also set in Liverpool, which Brophy described as "a city I am glad I no longer live in." It deals with a slum family in Liverpool's dockland and culminates in the arrest of the father, a seaman, on a murder charge. While awaiting trial he is imprisoned in Walton gaol. Another sordid novel with a Liverpool background is "City of Departures," in which three schoolboys make a pact to hold a reunion in their native Liverpool 25 years later.

Liverpool's slums have not lacked chroniclers, but there are hardly any literary studies of her merchants. There is no Liverpool "Babbitt." There is no lack of cotton brokers or sons of cotton brokers who have turned to literature, but few have considered Liverpool business life as a subject for their works. An exception was John Owen, whose "The Cotton Broker" narrates how a five shilling a week messenger boy made his fortune on the Liverpool Cotton Exchange, married well and acquired a large house "across the water." He commits an act of dishonesty, faces disgrace and is spiritually regenerated. Unfortunately, John Owen like many Liverpool authors, felt it necessary to slightly alter the names of Liverpool institutions in his novel, referring to the Adelphi Hotel as the Atlantic. "The Cotton Broker" was serialised in

John Brophy on the set with the stars of "Waterfront" filmed on location in Liverpool, c. 1950.

_____ . _____ I was asked to return to Lewis's for 12
months as Advertising Manager and at something like an
appropriate salary.

I spent twelve another year — 193 — in
Liverpool and enjoyed it but I was kept so busy I could do practically
no writing of my own. At the end of the twelve months the man
who had invited me back to Lewis's — J.R. Charter — had
left the firm and I did not feel that his successor was
enthusiastic for me to stay. Collin Brookes [then on the
Financial News or Financial Times] visited Liverpool
about that time. I met him at the Press Club and he helped
me make up my mind to try once again to earn a
living by writing books and essays and not by journalism. "I'll
help," he said — and he did. "Waterfront" published by
Cape in 1934 was my first big success with critics and
with the public.

As I see it in retrospect the final period of twelve
months I spent in Liverpool was a decisive point in my career as
an author if only because, out of what I observed and thought and felt
in Lewis's store, I obtained some of the raw material for "Waterfront,"
the first of my novels which came near to satisfying the
standards I set for myself.   John Brophy   7 Sept. 62.

Manuscript of John Brophy's autobiography.
(Brown Library, Liverpool)

the *Daily Post.* In many of Owen's other stories he used his knowledge of Merseyside, but he preferred to live in Felixstowe. The manuscripts for his two best known Merseyside novels "The Cotton Broker" and "The Beauty of the Ships" — are in the Picton Library.

A Liverpool businessman — Arthur Behrend — belongs to one of Liverpool's oldest shipping firms — Bahr, Behrend and Company. He wrote a best-selling thriller with a Liverpool background entitled "The House of the Spaniard." It was set in Wirral and was filmed.

Whereas Liverpool's own writers, like Hanley and Brophy, invented fictional names for their grim versions of Liverpool, and have little good to say for it other writers have found the port an inspiration and a centre for Romance.

Sir Hugh Walpole loved Liverpool. "I love this place and have done so ever since I was 20." Walpole worked with the Mersey Mission for Seamen for a year, narrating that he had "never known such terror as when walking up and down a dock trying to summon up the courage to ask a captain if he would like his sailors to have a service." While a King's Messenger during the first world war, he had often to sail from Liverpool to Petrograd and put up at the Adelphi. One night in 1917 when walking to his ship he fell into the icy water, and was rescued unconscious.

Another popular novelist during the long week-end between the wars was Francis Brett Young, who shipped as a medical officer on a Blue Funnel liner. His experiences gave him the background for "Sea Horses." He received £8 a month and his ship was the Kintuck. He stated that no ship had appealed to him as much as the Kintuck with her "beautiful lines and lovely teak decks."

In the period between the two world wars. Liverpool produced a crop of women novelists. Marguerite Steen used the slum of dockland as background to her "The Wise and Foolish Virgins.". She describes the squalor, but the picture is relieved by hope. Marguerite Steen has, however, chosen Bristol for the background of her more important novels. Winifred Duke preferred the name Salchester for her tales of middle-class Victorian life "Household Gods" and its continuation "Counterfeit" and the "Mart of Nations." She came from a quiet middle-class background, being the daughter of Canon

Duke, who was a curate of St. Mary's West Derby, 1883-9. She was educated at Belvedere School and was also fascinated by the horrors of Liverpool's streets. "The Stroke of Murder" gave an account of the Liverpool handcart murder for which George Ball was sentenced to death in Liverpool. She also wrote a fictional reconstruction of the Wallace murder case.

In an article in the *Daily Post*, Winifred Duke regretted that "civility has been exchanged for bluntness, abruptness for consideration and good manners, lack of time pleaded as excuse for failing to acknowledge a present or return some trivial service. We pride ourselves on having none of the small hypocrisies of the past era, yet we might still sweeten life by what seem little things."

The intellectual powers of another woman writer — May Sinclair (1870-1946) — attracted a high level of critical acclaim. Born in Rock Ferry, daughter of a Liverpool Merchant, May Sinclair produced novels, short stories, poetry, biography, studies and translations.

A major figure in the history of modern English Literature, the poet Wilfred Owen (1893-1918) also spent his formative years "over the water", in Birkenhead. Owen was only 25 when he died in action during the Great War and at that time his work was little known. Today, he is considered to be one of the outstanding poets of his generation and of this century.

Liverpool has also produced some distinguished critics and essayists in the 20th Century. Holbrook Jackson was born in Stanley Road, Liverpool. His career was mainly devoted to authorship, editing and journalism. Probably his best book was "The Eighteen Nineties." He also wrote a book on William Morris and the first book on Shaw. In 1945, he presented to the Picton Library some of his privately printed or out-of-print works. A comprehensive exhibition of his works was held in 1958 in the Rare Book Division of the Philadelphia Public Library.

Colin Brooks was educated at the Liverpool Institute and was for two years Organising Secretary for the League of Nations Union and a local journalist. He published his serious novels under the pseudonym Barnaby Brook and his detective tales and financial books under his own name. Perhaps his best books are "Wife to John" and "Prosperity Street."

James Laver, who was born in Liverpool, and was also

The poet Wilfred Owen killed in action in the 1914-18 war.
(Photograph by courtesy of Harold Owen)

educated at Liverpool Institute, has had an even more versatile career as a writer. He has recently presented two of the original manuscripts of his works to the Picton Library — that of his life of Whistler, and his serious philosophic poem, "Macrocosmos," which was broadcast by the B.B.C. His works include poetry, art criticism, the theatre, dress and costume, biographies, novels, translating short stories and a children's book. His verse satire, "A Stitch in Time," was published in a special edition by the Nonesuch Press and speedily became a collector's piece. Some of his earliest verses appeared in Fowler Wright's "Poets of Merseyside." When opening an exhibition in Liverpool in 1934 he stated that he would like to see a line of poets moving down Lime Street with sandwich boards carrying their best and second-best poems inscribed on them.

One of the few 20th century writers who remained in Liverpool was John Pride. His three long epics, "The Prophet," "Death" and "Life," were published by the *Daily Post and Echo*. His "Quair of Sonnets" was written, illustrated and edited by himself in the tradition of Blake. His poem, "The Mersey," runs as follows:

> *Mast and shroud in steam and cloud,*
> *Funnel and sail and spar,*
> *From the ports of the earth his vessels berth*
> *Loading his wharf with treasure and worth.*
> *Like traders from afar.*

Pride devoted much of his leisure to painting scenes of contemporary Liverpool for the Picton Library's collection of water colours documenting the city's history. In this connection, and as a poet, he is one of the few artists who loved Liverpool so much that he was content to remain in the city.

Chapter 10

The 20th Century (2): Malcolm Lowry; Nicholas Monsarrat; Alun Owen; other dramatists and novelists.

10

In the period since the Second World War ended Liverpool cannot complain at the lack of novelists, poets and dramatists prepared to write about the city. Not only have the great names from earlier generations continued to find inspiration in Liverpool, but the new generation of writers since the Second World War have probably written more about Liverpool than any other provincial city. Unfortunately, it is the vice and squalor of Liverpool which too often is reflected in this literature.

Of the considerable number of writers born in Liverpool, most have, as in previous generations, left the city. A notable example who has achieved a considerable posthumous reputation was Malcolm Lowry, son of a Liverpool cotton broker. He was born in New Brighton and published his first novel — "Ultramarine" — in 1933, inspired by his experiences as a deck hand on a Blue Funnel ship before going to Cambridge, The hero of the novel was born, like Lowry, in a middle class background on Merseyside, but ships on a Norwegian tramp. The crew mistrust him because of his superior class status, and the memory of his sweetheart in Wallasey prevents him from giving way enthusiastically to the temptations in the ports he visits, but he does get drunk. Clearly, Lowry was, as a young man, a misfit, and, like D.H. Lawrence, tried to "shed his sickness in books." He did not, however, shed his weakness for drink, which was the cause of his death in 1957. Lowry could not fit into his middle-class background and became a sailor and hobo, living for periods in the West Indies, Russia, China, Canada and Mexico, and plagued always by his excessive drinking. His principal work "Under the Volcano" has been claimed to be one of the

Manuscript of Nicholas Monsarrat's *The Cruel Sea*
(Brown Library, Liverpool)

Nicholas Monsarrat looks out over the River Mersey
(Photograph by courtesy of Liverpool Daily Post & Echo Ltd.)

great English novels of the century. It describes the last day on earth of a drunkard who had many of the characteristics of his author. When it was published in 1947 it was called a work of genius. It has been re-published in 1962 in the Penguin Modern Classics.

A collection of Lowry's short stories, "Hear Us O, Lord From Heaven Thy Dwelling Place," was issued in the same year. In "Under the Volcano" there is a description of Leasowe. "The smoke of freighters outward bound from Liverpool hung low on the horizon. There was a feeling of space and emptiness." Was not that the feeling Lowry tried to shed in his writing and which drove him to drink.

A better known and immensely more popular Liverpool novelist of the period is Nicholas Monsarrat, whose "Cruel Sea" was one of the best sellers of the generation and was inspired by his experiences on a corvette in the North Atlantic in the Liverpool Escort Force during the war. When "The Cruel Sea" was serialised in the *Liverpool Echo* Monsarrat stated that "In no other place could I rather see my book serialised than in Liverpool – my home town. We were in the harbour – in Albert Dock, very close to the Liver building – during that nightmare week of raids in 1941. By an odd coincidence my brother Denys (later killed in North Africa) was a gunner in the Liverpool Ack-Ack defences at the time, and my father was a group medical officer for Merseyside and district.

Liverpool as headquarters of the Western Approaches Command made an enormous contribution to the Battle of the Atlantic and thus many people reading the 'Cruel Sea' will know what I am talking about."

Monsarrat was born in Rodney Street, the birthplace of so many of Liverpool's authors, next door to the birthplace of Arthur Hugh Clough.

Liverpool's vice, like the sea, has not failed to attract chroniclers in the years following the second world war, notably in Alexander Baird's "The Micky-Hunters". Baird was educated at the Liverpool Institute, before going to Liverpool and Cambridge Universities. At Liverpool he won the Felicia Hemans prize for lyric verse. In the "Micky-Hunters" he describes three under-privileged boys from a special school in search of "mickies" – pigeons – in a bombed warehouse, where they see violence and death.

A similar tale of Liverpool street urchins in the tradition of "Her Benny" but without the sentiment is H. J. Cross's "No Language but a Cry". The author draws in this novel on his experiences as a Merseyside schoolmaster.

With the shrinking of the world as a unit as a result of the aeroplane, radio and television, and the emergence of new countries, literature has been increasingly preoccupied with race relations. Liverpool has had long experience of the intermingling of peoples, and has long ceased to be an English port. Her people are a nice amalgam of Irish, Welsh, Scotch, English, with important colonies from most parts of the world. Since the second world war, there has been some tendency amongst Liverpool's writers to take race relations as their theme, and in this respect they have pioneered a truer portrayal.

J.A. Jerome, who was a journalist on the Liverpool *Daily Post and Echo*, has given in "Chinese White" a picture of the Chinese in Liverpool, which avoids most of the characteristics of sensational novels of opium dens and dope peddling.

There is, it is true, murder and vendetta, and the "blitz", but his characters are human beings. A Liverpool-born author, Bernard Ash, has given in "Omega Street" a study of a Russian watchmaker in Liverpool.

Since the Second World War, a number of Merseyside writers have made notable contributions to television drama, and the image they present of Liverpool is the same amalgam of the sea and vice which characterises its novels. Of Liverpool as a civilised city, there is hardly any mention. Cyril Abraham in "Ice Blink" and "Five Bells for Logan" has drawn upon his experiences in the Merchant Navy after leaving the Liverpool Collegiate. Henry Livings, who spent two years reading modern languages at Liverpool University, has portrayed in "Jack's Horrible Luck" a most sordid and horrible Liverpool. But the outstanding television dramatist to portray Merseyside is Alun Owen, who has loaned some of his manuscripts for the exhibition "Liverpool and Literature" in the Picton Library.

There is nothing "literary" about Owen. He left school at 15 and confesses that he always had trouble with his spelling — he spells Saturday Saterday. But he is a force in literature.

Alun Owen (left) pictured in Liverpool with the author, George Chandler. *(Photograph by courtesy of Liverpool Daily Post & Echo Ltd.)*

And no harm been done no harm at all
                    her mother's
Around her presses ~~the~~ eating love,
         its tears denying her any robbing ease,
blackmailing her into to silence,

Out now, to the kitchen, collect the plates,
July will be hot, its languor will heal.
August's the green sea and the holy voyage,
soft voices and the busy gnats, orange colored
tea ~~with~~ and soda bread.   September's the
Sale, a bargain bought, the long day's work
and smoke in the Park. But Please God,
make October easy. Our lady keep her busy
give her full hands or a dead heart in the ~~~~,
~~silver-grey~~ lonely grey days of October.

     ∆ But now it is June, the sun helps
Fathers hands into their pockets, it sends boys
running for after-lunch ice cream in
cake howls. Off-licenses sell pints or quarts,
the streets will empty and bees or horseflies
will ~~roam~~ weave in the Park.

Manuscript of Alun Owen's *Progress to the Park*

Although he is pre-occupied with the sordid, his vision and style are more distinctively Liverpudlian than that of any other writer of the past or present. He won a prize for the best teleplay of 1961 awarded by the Television and screen-writers Guild with "The Rose Affair." In 1960 he won a TV playwright award with three plays — "No Trams to Lime Street," "After the Funeral," and "Lena oh, my Lena." He has also written a stage play "Progress to the Park." Alun Owen was born in Menai. His father was a merchant seaman who moved to Liverpool when Alun was eight. He married at the early age of 16, and his wife types his manuscripts and drives his car. He worked in repertory as an assistant stage manager, and was a Bevin Boy during the war. Afterwards he held a great variety of posts — ship's steward, lorry driver's mate, actor, waiter, etc. His Welsh background and his wide experience of live have given him an uncanny ear for Liverpool, Northern and Welsh speech rhythms. He has done for Mersey-side a little of what O'Casey did for Ireland, but his achievement from one point of view greater.

There is a naturally poetic turn of expression amongst the Irish, as there is indeed, amongst the Welsh. Scouse has hitherto not been considered to have a poetic quality. It has a quickness and readiness which has enabled Liverpool to produce an unrivalled range of comedians, but before Owen it was never used with such poetic intensity.

To some extent the medium of television has assisted Owen to discover the poetic quality of Scouse. He has the vigour and liveliness which Liverpool possesses in great measure, and which arises from the conflicts within the City itself; between Irish and English, between Welsh and Scot, between Pro-testant and Catholic, between the middle-class and working class. Owen has realised that a fully worked out plot is not necessary. What matters is the intensity of the incident or the atmosphere. In boldly taking as his theme the conflicts in Liverpool, Owen hopes that by exposing them in compelling language he will alleviate them. Whether he will alleviate them is problematical. What is undeniable is that he has exposed them memorably and has strikingly widened the literary image of Liverpool.

Alun Owen wrote the book of the musical "Maggie May" which made use of Liverpool speech rhythms and a Liverpool

John McGrath *(Photograph by courtesy of Liverpool Daily Post & Echo Ltd.)*

Jeville Smith
Photograph by courtesy of iverpool Daily Post & :cho Ltd.)

setting. He also scripted a film for the Beatles and has gone on to reinforce his considerable reputation with plays for the theatre and television.

Primarily through the medium of television, a number of Liverpool-born dramatists have found a wider audience in recent years. They include A.E. Whitehead, John McGrath, Neville Smith, Julia Jones and Eric Coltart.

Chapter 11

Contemporary Poetry: The Mersey Sound and the
"Mainstream" revival.

One of the Beatles, John Lennon, wrote a modernistic best seller, but he was not part of the movement which gave a new dimension to the phrase "Mersey Sound" by extending its meaning to cover popular poetry. The best known of the "pop" poets were Adrian Henri, Roger McGough and Brian Patten, whose poems were published in 1967 in *The Mersey Sound*.

Some of their work had appeared earlier in *The Liverpool Scene*, edited by Edward Lucie-Smith, in which Alan Ginsberg, the American "hippie" poet, claimed that Liverpool was at that moment "the centre of consciousness of the human universe"! If one accepts that the problems of city life are centres of human consciousness, there is some point in this extravagant claim.

The Liverpool 8 poets reflected the city environment, employing simple language, often in an amusing way, to capture the interest of a wide audience. They became entertainers in their own right, reading, at first in pubs, and later in concert halls. Adrian Henri's poem on the opening of the Catholic·Metropolitan Cathedral is typical:

"A new cathedral at the end of Hope Street, ex-government surplus from Cape Kennedy ready to blast off taking a million Catholics to a heaven free from Orangemen . . . wind blowing in hard from Pierhead bringing the smell of breweries and engine oil from ferry boats."

Roger McGough, perhaps better known for his sharp wit, wrote in the same volume:

"Liverpool on the River Mersey, Noble city, how I shiver,
With pride at the thought of your history."

Brian Patten, whose work stands up better on the printed page, developed a more personal lyrical style and became Liverpool's "best selling" poet with several important collections to his name. The individual talents of Henry Graham and Matt Simpson also emerged during the sixties.

Although the Mersey sound attracted considerable attention, especially among the young, it made little impact on the mainstream of poetry, even on Merseyside. Liverpool is not only experimentalist, but also has a deep respect for timeless values and universal themes.

In 1973, reacting against the parochialism of existing literary coteries, Trevor Kneale launched in Liverpool, *Meridian,* a new poetry magazine which has established a national reputation. Kneale's editorial commitment to "sensibility and craftsmanship" informs his own poetry:

> *"Remembering it green*
> *before trees tumbled,*
> *rubble stopped dubs and ditches,*
> *before levelling of ploughed fields:*
> *reflective water-meadows*
> *gone blind under concrete."*

In the early seventies there has been a resurgence of mainstream poetry in Liverpool at a time when the City appeared to be lagging behind others, bogged down, perhaps, by the pervasive "pop" influence of the previous decade.

Among local poets whose reputations have grown in this new climate are John Barron Mays, whose first collection *"An Earthquake Somewhere Else"* was well received, and Gladys Mary Coles, winner of the 1971 Felicia Hemans Prize, and a number of national poetry awards. Mrs. Coles, is also researching and writing a definitive life of Mary Webb, a major literary biography.

In the mid-seventies other individuals and organisations, including the Merseyside Arts Association, have become involved in a series of new poetry projects. In addition to encouraging local poets of enduring quality, this activity promises to put Liverpool firmly on the international poetry map.